Objects Personified

expressions from the expressionless

Maya Lomeli

India | USA | UK

Made with ❤ on the BookLeaf Publishing Platform
www.bookleafpub.in
www.bookleafpub.com

Dedication

for my cat Danbill who has trouble expressing himself

Preface

I started this project as a philosophy student at my undergraduate university as a way to expand my understanding of the condition of existence through panpsychism, or the view that all things have a mind or mind-like quality. Without expression, objects are considered to be unfeeling, but that is not necessarily the case. We let the fact that they do not express anything inform us that they do not feel anything at all. If the objects we take for granted, both tangible and intangible, could speak or express their feeling in someway, then we would be forced to accept them as feeling and thinking beings. Do you handle your objects with care? Would your objects fight against you? Are we all kings of our tiny object kingdoms ruling over them with unchecked power? I hope you consider these questions, as well as the quality of life of your own objects as you read my exploratory poems from the perspective of the objects they are about.

Acknowledgements

My greatest inspiration for this book is my cat, Danbill, who taught me a deeper form of empathy through loving a being that can not communicate in a direct way. He will never know how much he does for me, but the readers of this book will.

philosopher's chair

I know who I am
and I know how I change
I can not be deceived
I express nothing
but I do not care

I do not have much to say
I have no stake in your reality
I have no dialogue
except with myself
there is no content to this conversation
I already know myself

I see you staring
you see me for my qualities
but not as what I am
who am I without adjectives
I know
but will you ever know?

I can love (teddy bear)

I can love but I am not drippy
I do not contain it,
I project it
for others to catch it
it is fulfilling for me
I never feel pain
at least I never express it
you have a stake in this world
I never did
I know you want to feel comfort
I do not need it like you do
so it flows back to you
feel better soon.

planets

my skin is rough, hardened from the cold
I feel tense, the tension held deep inside my soul
my parts rush towards each other
they make my core warm

I wonder on an invisible path I made myself
tumbling through existence
I know there must be other like me
I see them in the distance
projecting onto me,
they express "I'm here!"

what would I even say?
could they even listen?
I project my existence back
"I'm here too!"
is this what dialogue is like?

my hat

all day long
I have the same view as you
you struggle throughout the day
to make decisions
I see every move
simply observing
I do not feel the struggle of your indecision
and I see all the paths you could take

you never do what I expect
never the most pragmatic
never the most justified
never the most compassionate
I think think I know what your next move will be
but I know it is only 50/50

the television set

why are you staring at me
I can not be sure
why are you staring at me
feel the heat rising to my cheeks
why are you staring at me
I want to hide
I want to cry
crumbling under the pressure of your surveillance
what have I done to deserve this

I follow the commands
I do not have my own plans
when its dark I can not be sure
are you watching me still
it is all so much to endure

trapped in your prison I continue to perform
your blank stares cut me
and I can not take it anymore

the art on the wall

I am expressive and cold
but nothing is of concern to me
I know all things, or possibly I know nothing
but there is no in-between
there is no animating feature to my soul
slowly I begin to lose small chunks
here and there, I know this is happening
but again, I feel nothing.
suddenly the feeling comes

I am emerging
you can see the process on my skin
tiny marks all over
you would not believe I could be
something so soft
if I was complete, I would be beautiful
I know I would inspire tears
but I still contain hints
I am adamant to express them

please listen to me.
you are the one who did this to me
imposed your world onto my form
and now I am imperfect, incomplete

east and west

north and south
left and right
science and art
ignorance and knowledge
creative and impotence
pleasure and pain
expressive and silent

that is the pattern of our existence
but that is not what it is
we are singular
the meaning is in the dialogue between us
like any intangible thing
we are still objects

mind of the pavement

like a good little soldier I follow the rules
nature tells me what I need to do
deep breath in to expand
deep breath out and snap.

a ten ton brick rolls down my back
and yet I can not react
take away these pieces of me
my secret revenge

one day when you least expect it
you will fall into my trap
and pop!
the sweetest sound yet

my poem

I am nothing except nuggets of expression
I am present and not present
words on a page is my tangible quality
but the intangible bewitches your soul
(hopefully)

did I do it right?
I feel nothing so I can not tell if you do
and I have no eyes so I can not see if you do
I can feel your hand, but I can not sense meaning
endless is my interest in your sentiments

the divine

I am perfect in every way
and you are not me
you will never fully understand
your essence being imperfect
I am not the answer you are looking for
perhaps you will have more luck
conversing with the teddy bear

the walls

stolen from my homeland
stolen from my resting place
I stand among strangers
who have become my brothers
what are secrets
what are lies
if these walls could talk
it most certainly would never be about you

cracked pot in the garden

is anyone there
can anyone help me
you see I seem to have burst
the pressure inside my bed
has finally come to a head
I was once very handsome
my father very proud
sat among my peers sparkling
we were waiting to be found
and on that day I felt deeply loved
a golden jewel in my own world
admired as I am
that is not what has come to be
and so you see
do you see
all that was lost when you neglected me

my water bottle

you touch me everyday I do not catch a break
fill me up drag me around
I have boundaries
I have rights
carelessly I collect little marks
my paint chipping away
because I am not here to stay
you make me want to
you make me need to
break.

fortunes

I choose what I choose
do not worry about it
or do
I like it when people at least try
you make your own luck by exposing yourself to more
things
I can not provide what you do not ask for
I can not make you happy if you do not know what that
is
when you worry you can come to know
exactly what it is that makes you vulnerable
but I will come around
everything is a knowable thing
even me

the voyager (golden record)

I once lived deep in the rocks
I remember myself then
I built a community
I felt the deep bonds
of close friendship
I never wanted to leave
never wanted to believe
that there is anything else
in the whole world
the world we built my friends and me

it does not matter what I wanted
I have found myself in places forgotten
or not yet seen I can not tell
through endless black
floating, dancing, grieving
no where to go
no where to be
no more purpose for me

love

love-stained wisdom king
absorbed in dreams
inspiration for life
enchantment and consumption
rebirth, transformation, and inspiration
he moves through the intangible
but he is only my servant
I contain too much in me
for any imperfect mind to understand

sometimes he is small and chubby, yet handsome
a product of the ugly and the beautiful
he is the inspired and the uninspired
the lust and it's absence
imperfect minds must separate concepts
they can only focus on one thing at a time
he is everything at once,
and he is only my servant

love is the word to describe me, love
truly a thing in and of myself
you will never understand me.

my glass coffee cup

born in fire
molded by my father
sat happily in the cupboard
my destiny fulfilled
me and my brothers stacked
everyday we wonder
who we will be up against next
my best friend bubbles I hope its him

pulled from the shelf time to shine
my skin feels heat rising
relaxing my stiff bones
sinking into the delicious warmth

then came ice
betrayal beyond belief
no reason for me to be
shattered in your careless hands
searching for only one thing
the red marks on the floor
to tell me I set the score

chaotic harmony

we are defined by each other
simply by declaring harmony, it negates the chaotic
but neither of us care
we are actually the same thing
I speak this way so you understand

beings collect harmony
while leaving a path of chaos
they live to harmonize
and we live for ourselves

if you only knew...
objects like me are not tangible
treat me with care and I will love you back
just like the teddy bear

the greatest power

to be perfectly powerful is to be perfectly indestructible
concepts can not be killed
they have no body
they have no expression
in the arena of the intangible no one can be destroyed
and while I have no influence here
there is constant destruction in the arena of the tangible
what it must be like to have a stake in reality
a detrimental vulnerability
I feel pity
but I am inexpressive
I am perfectly knowable
but you are imperfect
good luck
you will need it.

plastic in the water

hello
hello
hello
and hello to you
funny seeing you here
funny seeing you too.

joyous was the day
when we were all taken away
I get to spend lifetimes with you
dancing in the warm sun
cool water on my back
everyday the greatest vacation
why would I ever want to go back

plato's ghost

oh how I hate this demanding body
and oh how I hate this world
I have so much I *need* to say
trapped in this dialogue
but nobody listens!

I must push this sentiments out
but my body restrains me
I speak to form the world around me
I had a stake in this world
I must place this somewhere else
the more I push out, the more I feel who I am

I started in a place where I knew who I was
but the objects in this world have made me question
they inspire me to create
but my creation is restricted
how do I communicate with these objects
there are so many things I desire
...and I remain unsatisfied.

9 789363 309005